Cooper Kupp: The Inspiring Story of One of Football's Star Wide Receivers

An Unauthorized Biography

By: Clayton Geoffreys

Table of Contents

Foreword

Since being drafted in the third round of the 2017 NFL Draft, Cooper Kupp has accomplished quite a lot in his professional football career. At the time of this writing, Kupp won the Offensive Player of the Year Award in 2021 and was named Super Bowl MVP LVI. In the same year, he was recognized as the fourth player since the AFL-NFL Merger to lead the league in receptions, receiving yards and receiving touchdowns. It's crazy to think that at one point in his life, Cooper didn't even have a football scholarship offer (he received one several weeks after having already played the final game of his senior season). Thank you for purchasing *Cooper Kupp: The Inspiring Story of One of Football's Star Wide Receivers*. In this unauthorized biography, we will learn Cooper Kupp's incredible life story and impact on the game of football. Hope you enjoy and if you do, please do not forget to leave a review!

Also, check out my website at claytongeoffreys.com to join my exclusive list where I let you know about my latest books. To thank you for your purchase, you can go to my site to download a free copy of *33 Life Lessons: Success Principles, Career Advice & Habits of Successful People.* In the book, you'll learn from some of the greatest thought leaders of different industries on what it takes to become successful and how to live a great life.

Cheers,

Clayton Geoffreys

Visit me at www.claytongeoffreys.com

Introduction

Predicting a future NFL player is nearly impossible. There are more than 1.1 million high school students who play football every year. Out of all of those who play, only a few thousand will end up playing in college. And of the thousands who play college football, only approximately 260 will be drafted into the NFL.

There are so many factors outside of a player's control that could interrupt the journey from high school to the NFL.

Many players' careers end because they simply are not good enough. For those who have talent, sometimes injuries can block their path. Other times, it is their work ethic or an inability to raise their mental game to match the level of other players.

And because it is impossible to know what is in someone's heart and mind, sometimes great players are overlooked. They aren't heavily recruited out of high school because their talents are not fully recognized or they get passed on in the draft because they are not seen as a viable risk.

But sometimes, it is those very players who feel they have something to prove to the world that end up being the best. For example, Tom Brady. He has been proving doubters wrong for more than 20 years and now has seven Super Bowl titles.

Tom Brady did not come from some small school in the middle of nowhere, however. He went to Michigan. But there are also a number of small-time athletes who were not recruited out of high school, ended up at FCS schools, and *still* made an impact on the NFL.

Defensive ends Howie Long (Villanova), Richard Dent (Tennessee State), and Michael Strahan (Texas Southern) all played at small schools and still made the Hall of Fame. Another prime example of a player who was overlooked coming out of high school was Jerry Rice.

Former MVP quarterbacks Steve McNair and Kurt Warner were both overlooked coming out of high school and went on to have great careers, including leading their teams to the Super Bowl. In Warner's case, even winning one.

Rice, meanwhile, was the son of a bricklayer, and helping his dad move those bricks helped develop the strength in his hands. He would end up at Mississippi Valley State, where he set several FCS receiving records. After that, it was on to the San Francisco 49ers and eventually, the Pro Football Hall of Fame. When the conversation is about legendary NFL receivers, Rice will always be one of the first names that come up.

The records that Rice set while he was playing in the FCS were eventually broken by none other than Cooper Kupp. Like most of the other players mentioned, Kupp was overlooked coming out of high school and only ended up with two FCS scholarship offers.

Kupp had a different path to NFL stardom and Super Bowl MVP status than Rice. Cooper Kupp actually comes from a long line of NFL players. The Kupps are one of five venerated families in the history of the league to have three generations of family members play in the NFL. Kupp's grandfather, Jake, was a Pro Bowl offensive lineman for the Saints, among other teams. Jake ended up blocking for Archie Manning, a relationship that would benefit his grandson in later years.

Kupp's father, Craig, was drafted by the New York Giants and also played for the Cardinals and Cowboys as well as in the World Football League. Indeed, the Kupp family was continually around football. Jake would allow his grandchildren to try on his old helmets and run around the house wearing them. The grandkids would only stop after one of them inevitably ran into a wall.

Having a former quarterback as a father also certainly helped Cooper's development as a receiver. His father would have him run patterns outside, and when it got too cold, they would play catch on a small patch of rug in the family's living room.

Furthermore, Cooper's mother, Karin, was also an athlete. She participated in cross-fit races and was an All-American soccer player at Pacific Lutheran University, where she met Craig.

Yes, athletics surrounded the Kupp family. Cooper started playing baseball but quickly switched over to football after watching a football team practicing in the outfield near his baseball field. But before heading to high school, Cooper also started playing basketball. He was a decent basketball player but did it more for the training and agility he learned from the sport.

When it came time for high school, Cooper Kupp had his choice of very good schools. The family lived on the west side of Yakima, Washington. But he chose to go to A.C. Davis High School, which was located on the poorer east side of town.

With Cooper and his friends at Davis, the team had its first winning season in more than two decades. Kupp played both football and basketball at the school. In his senior season, he was all-state in football as both a receiver and a defensive back. He also helped the Davis basketball team win a state championship in his senior year.

By his senior season, Cooper Kupp was one of the best receivers in the state of Washington, but he still did not have a scholarship offer. His grandfather even contacted the University of Washington on his behalf, but they passed on him.

Finally, in the middle of basketball season during his senior year, he received his first scholarship offer from

Idaho State University. And then his second came from Eastern Washington University. The future Super Bowl MVP had only two college scholarship offers and decided to attend EWU.

Cooper was forging another life-changing relationship at this time as well. Before he left for college, he met a young woman named Anna Croskrey at a track meet. The two instantly fell in love. She was headed off to the University of Arkansas on a track scholarship. Within three years, though, they would be married. They are still married today and have two sons together.

Kupp had to redshirt his freshman year at EWU. During his redshirt freshman season, Kupp assaulted the FCS record books. He set a new FCS freshman record for receptions, touchdowns, and receiving yards. He received the Jerry Rice Award as the top freshman in the FCS, and he was named first team All-American.

Kupp continued his assault on the record books for his next three seasons at Eastern Washington. Each year he was with the Eagles, he set new school records for receptions and receiving yards. In his junior season, he won the Walter Payton Award as the top FCS player.

After marrying Anna during his redshirt sophomore year, she transferred to EWU, and the two would eventually graduate together. Despite being one of the best receivers in the nation, Kupp played for all four years of his eligibility with the Eagles.

By the end of his senior season, Cooper Kupp was one of the most decorated receivers in the history of college football. He was a four-time All-American and set the record for the most receiving yards in the history of college football.

Yet, despite setting numerous records, Kupp was still not considered a top draft prospect for the NFL. He performed well at the Senior Bowl, but two rounds of the draft passed, and he still did not hear his name called.

Finally, the Los Angeles Rams selected Kupp with the fifth pick in the third round of the draft. The Rams had a crowded receiver room, but Kupp had a solid rookie season under new head coach Sean McVay. Kupp got off to a solid start during his second year, but he tore his ACL in Week 10 against Seattle.

After Kupp went out with his injury, the Rams would go on to lose the Super Bowl to the New England Patriots 13-3. Sadly, Kupp could only watch from the sidelines.

Cooper had always been a gym rat, but now he was forced to spend the entire offseason rehabbing his injured knee. He continued to strengthen his upper body, even while his knee was healing. Once he was cleared, Kupp spent months getting himself back into football shape.

Upon his return to the lineup, Cooper became a dominant force for the Rams. He led the team in receptions, receiving yards, and touchdowns for the first time in his career. He followed that up by leading the team in receptions and receiving yards in 2020.

During the offseason, the Rams traded for quarterback Matthew Stafford. Kupp and Stafford immediately began to form a connection off the field that would quickly show up on the field.

In 2021, Cooper Kupp became just the fourth player in the history of the NFL to lead the league in catches, receiving yards, and touchdowns. He had one of the greatest seasons in the history of the NFL.

The Rams won the NFC West and defeated the Arizona Cardinals in the opening round of the playoffs. In the Divisional Round, the Rams found themselves tied with the Buccaneers with 42 seconds remaining in the game. On the final drive, Kupp caught two passes to get the ball down to the Bucs' 12-yard line to set up the game-winning field goal.

In the NFC Championship game, the Rams faced off against the 49ers. At that point, San Fran had won six straight against LA. Kupp scored the Rams only two touchdowns as LA finally knocked off San Fran 20-17.

In the Super Bowl, fellow receiver Odell Beckham Jr. tore his ACL, which allowed the Cincinnati Bengals to double-team Kupp. He caught a touchdown in the first half, but in the second and third quarters, he only had two receptions. On the final drive of the game, Kupp and Stafford connected on four passes for 39 yards, including the game-winning touchdown catch.

With that catch, Cooper Kupp became just the eighth receiver in history to win the Super Bowl MVP Award.

Following the Super Bowl victory, the Rams had a serious hangover. Although struggles following a Super Bowl win are quite common, LA became the worst defending Super Bowl Champion in the history of the NFL. Injuries helped to define and derail the Rams' season, as Stafford and star defensive lineman Aaron Donald both missed time with injuries.

Kupp was off to a great season but suffered a high ankle sprain in Week 10 against Arizona. The injury would require surgery, and he missed the remainder of the season. It was the second time in his NFL career that Kupp missed eight or more games in a season.

Despite those unfortunate injuries, Cooper Kupp has proven himself to be one of the best receivers in the NFL. He has proven he can bounce back from adversity and come back even better.

Now, at only 30 years of age, Kupp has the opportunity to establish himself as one of the greatest receivers in history. He has already done it at the college level, and now, he's working his way through the NFL.

The high school kid that no FBS colleges wanted, who only had two scholarships to FCS schools, is now a $100-million receiver in the NFL and a Super Bowl MVP. It is an incredible journey that continues to amaze, and an incredible story to tell.

Chapter 1: Childhood & High School

Washington State is not exactly a hotbed of high school football. The state will produce between 25-30 FBS players every year, far below other states with similar populations like Tennessee and Arizona.

But for the Kupp family, Washington is home and has been for generations. The family's roots in Washington football started with Cooper's grandfather, Jake Kupp.

Jake grew up on a farm in Yakima Valley. The family did not have very much money, so his mother told him to read books as a way to visualize faraway worlds. Jake says that his mother wanted to broaden his outlook beyond "what my 'normal' capacity would be."[i]

At night, Jake would settle under a peach tree and visualize himself playing for the New York Yankees. He knew he wanted to be a professional athlete, but he was a little off on the sport.

The idea of dreaming and visualizing one beyond their current circumstances was something that was passed down through generations in the Kupp family. It would help each generation see beyond the poverty in the Yakima Valley and ultimately propel them to the highest levels of football.

Jake was a star at the University of Washington, playing in two Rose Bowls with the Huskies. After college, he went on to play guard for the New Orleans Saints and Dallas Cowboys.

While playing for the Saints, he would be a three-time offensive captain and make one Pro Bowl. He had the opportunity to block for Archie Manning, and the two became friends. It is a friendship that lasts to this day.

It is a great football coincidence that the eldest Manning and the eldest Kupp played together. Kupp would go on to have three generations of his family play in the Super Bowl, while Manning is hoping that he will have his third generation coming soon with grandson Arch. Between the two families, they have four Super Bowl MVPs, but none for the patriarchs, as they played for the lowly Saints.

After his career ended, Jake returned to Washington to raise his children with his wife, Carla. Both Jake and Carla have brothers who played both high school and college football in Washington. Their roots run deep in the Yakima Valley.

His son, Craig, played at Pacific Lutheran University, where he met his wife, Karin. She was an All-American soccer player, while he was an All-American football player. Karin's father was a high school football coach in the area as well.

"I was pretty much used to football by the time I met Craig," Karin said. "And obviously I still am."[ii]

Craig was eventually drafted by the New York Giants before playing for the Phoenix Cardinals and Dallas Cowboys. He eventually played for two separate teams in the now-defunct World Football League.

There have been hundreds of father/son duos who have played in the NFL, but what would make this family remarkable would be if they could somehow get a third generation into the league. That's where Cooper comes in.

Cooper Kupp was born on June 15, 1993, in Yakima, Washington. Early in his life, he harnessed that determination and visualization that had propelled his father and grandfather to the NFL. His father would frequently tell him that he could be anything that he wanted to be in life, while his grandfather would read him *The Little Engine that Could.*

His mother started running marathons, teaching fitness boot camps, and competing in extreme endurance races after her soccer career was over. Cooper started tagging along to events with his mother and working out with her at a young age. When he was in his early teens, he even competed in a mini-triathlon.

Like most kids who are too young to play football, Cooper excelled at baseball. But when he was nine years old, a youth football team was practicing in the outfield near where Cooper's baseball team was practicing. He wandered over to take a look and never went back. For the Kupp family, football was everything.

"We don't have many family gatherings where there isn't a football around somewhere," Cooper said.[iii]

Having a former NFL quarterback for a father also helped in Cooper's development as a player and a receiver. Every night, when Craig would get home from work, the pair had a ritual. If the weather cooperated, they would head outside, and Cooper would run routes with his dad firing passes to him.

"I was so lucky," Cooper said. "I had an NFL quarterback as my wide receiver coach growing up. If I didn't run a double move right, my dad would let me know about it."[iv]

When the weather didn't cooperate, the father and son had an indoor ritual. There was a roughly 10-yard piece of space between the front door and the dining room table in the Kupp house. Cooper would rehearse his routes over and over again on that small piece of his childhood home.

"He'd (Craig) come home from work, he'd get down on his knees and I'd run back and forth and catch as many touchdowns as I could," Cooper said. "That's what we would do."[v]

Cooper also began to play basketball when he was a kid, not because he was particularly good at it or big for his size but because he thought it would help him be more agile at receiver. He also started wearing ankle weights as he went about his day-to-day activities to strengthen his legs.

It was all part of the vision that Cooper had for himself. He had seen both his father and grandfather play in the NFL, and even at a young age, he believed that he would one day play in the league as well. All the while, his family stood behind him and believed that he would one day make it.

"It's very cool to be a part of the family I have, not just from the athletics side of things, but also just the mentors that are in my family," Cooper said. "The opportunity to look up to them has been pretty special, and to share that passion too. I think that's the coolest part to have that connection, that my grandparents, my parents, and my brothers and sisters all have that shared passion."[vi]

But his family was not just about football. Every Sunday, the Kupp family, all of them, went to church together and would usually eat a big meal together. It was a chance for everyone to be together at Jake and Carla's house. But there were always special moments when Cooper and his siblings could sneak down to the basement to play with their grandfather's memorabilia from his playing days.

"When I was little, we called my grandfather Bumpa," Cooper said. "So Bumpa had a mancave in his basement and he had all the team MVP trophies and stuff like that down there. It was really cool to be able to look at all of that. To us, he was Bumpa first and NFL All-Pro second."[vii]

Bumpa would encourage the kids to try on his helmets from his playing days. Cooper and his siblings would run around the house with the large helmets on until one of them would run into a wall headfirst.

When it came time for high school, Cooper had to make a tough decision. Yakima is a city of roughly 93,000 people. Like most cities, there are parts that are quintessentially Washington, but others that represent the worst of America. There are apple orchards and wineries on the side of town where Cooper and his family lived, but poverty, gang violence, and drugs were the norm on the other side of the city.

There were three schools that Cooper could attend. Both Eisenhower and West Valley were located on the more affluent west side of the city. A.C. Davis High School was located downtown and was the oldest school in the city.

The Kupp family lived on the west side of town, and Cooper was supposed to attend Eisenhower High School. But Davis did have two advantages. The school introduced an International Baccalaureate program, which interested Cooper, and two of his friends and teammates attended Davis.

In the end, Cooper chose to commute across the city and attend Davis. But he was not recruited to the school for his football ability. Two of his teammates, who were also incoming freshmen, were already stars in Yakima, David Trimble and Deion Wright.

At the time, Cooper was only five foot five, but the coaches at Davis had already heard about his ability and work ethic.

"I kept hearing about this kid," Former Davis offensive coordinator and current head coach Jay Dumas said. "He was different from everybody else in what he was trying to get out of the game, super smart. But you never know."[viii]

Weighing only 115 pounds, Cooper hit the weight room when he got to high school. He became friends with custodians at the school so that he could stay later or arrive early for weight training. While other football players would look at themselves in the mirror, Cooper was more interested in the process and making himself better.

Despite being so small, Cooper refused to gain weight by eating junk food. When the team bus would stop at Burger King or McDonald's on the way home from games, Cooper would watch as his teammates ate their fast food.

Cooper did not play varsity in either basketball or football as a freshman, but by the start of his sophomore year, he had gained both weight and height and was ready to get on the field.

Just before the season started, Cooper found Dumas and asked him a strange question. He asked if Dumas thought he could play college football.

"Yes, maybe," Dumas responded. "In the back of my mind, I thought he'd probably play at Central Washington." Dumas was referring to the nearby Division II school.[ix]

But the questions kept coming from Cooper. He asked Dumas if he thought that he could play in the NFL. It was an outlandish question coming from a kid who had never played varsity football in high school and who, at the time, was not even six feet tall. But Cooper continued. He confessed that his goal in life wasn't just to play in the NFL, but he wanted to make it all the way to the Pro Football Hall of Fame, a feat that neither his father nor grandfather had achieved.[x]

To his credit, Dumas did not shoot down Cooper's dreams but told him to keep working at it. It was just a sign of the goals that Cooper would one day achieve.

Cooper started on the varsity as a sophomore, catching 19 passes for 230 yards. During his junior season, he began to become a star in the Yakima area, catching 31 passes for 811 yards and 7 touchdowns.[xi]

It was not necessarily the touchdowns he caught but the ones he missed that his former head coach Rick Clark remembers.

"We were playing Wenatchee and we were very young," Clark said. "Coop dropped two balls in the end zone and took it really hard, and after he wouldn't leave practice until he caught about 100 balls."[xii]

By his senior season, Cooper was a two-year starter in both football and basketball. He had a dominant senior season on the football field. He had 60 catches for 1,059 yards and 18 touchdowns. He also rushed for another four touchdowns, bringing his total to a school-record of 22 scores.[xiii]

For the first time since the 1960s, Davis had back-to-back winning seasons and made the playoffs during Cooper's senior year. Davis had a great chance of winning the game against Mead, but in the first quarter, Davis' quarterback left the game with an injury. Cooper played the final three-quarters of the game at quarterback, going 5-10 for 76 yards. Despite never having played the position, he was able to play admirably in the team's biggest game of the season.

"He was the hardest worker, but he was smart, like another coach on the field, and always seemed to be in the right place at the right time," Scott Spruill, a longtime sportswriter at the *Yakima Herald* newspaper said.[xiv]

Despite being all-state at both wide receiver and defensive back, Cooper did not receive any scholarship offers during the regular season. Cooper wanted to go to Yale, and with a 4.0 GPA, he had the grades, and he believed that he could play at the Ivy League school.

The coach from Yale who was recruiting Cooper showed up at one of his games with his father and Cooper believed that this was a good sign.

"The coach that was recruiting me, his dad was actually at a game," Cooper said. "So, I felt like 'Okay, this is going to be a thing for me. I have a good shot at going here.' That week, after that first game, the coach called me and said that they were going a different direction with it. So, right in the middle of the season, I lost the only interest that I had."[xv]

With no college offers, Cooper finished up his football season and went right into basketball season. On the basketball court, Cooper wasn't a star, but he did it to stay in shape for football and to be with his friends.

"They changed the whole dynamic, the whole attitude," basketball coach Eli Juarez said about Kupp and his friends. "They said 'we're going to get to class, we're going to work hard.' Coop did all the little things. That great screen, that critical basket. Always at the right place at the right time."[xvi]

Despite being in basketball season, Cooper kept up the hope that he would get a football scholarship. His family hired a recruiting service to help get his name out. He sent tapes to as many coaches as he could find and he even had his grandfather make some calls to Washington, his alma mater, on his grandson's behalf.

"It was tough," Cooper said. "There's no feeling like that. I believed that I could play at the next level, but there is that voice in the back of your head saying, 'Well, right now no one else thinks that you can.' You know? But it didn't change my idea."[xvii]

Finally, a few weeks into basketball season, he got his first scholarship offer from Idaho State University. Another one quickly followed from Eastern Washington University. After taking some time to think over the two offers, Cooper decided that he would take his talents to EWU.

But before he could leave for college, Cooper had some unfinished business. He helped guide his basketball team to a Washington state championship with a 28-4 record.

Later in his senior year, Cooper was running track to help with his speed. At a track meet, he would meet Anna Croskrey. The two immediately hit it off, and despite going to different schools and both being seniors, they started dating.

"I knew that she was the one that I wanted to marry when we had first met back in high school," Cooper said. "I told my mom the day I met her, 'I'm going to marry this girl.'"xviii

There was a slight problem with Cooper's plan to marry Anna. She was on her way to the University of Arkansas on a track scholarship, and Cooper was headed to Eastern Washington.

31

But despite the distance between them, they would eventually end up at the same college and later in life get married.

Despite only having two college scholarship offers, Cooper Kupp was on his way to play receiver at Eastern Washington University.

Chapter 2: Eastern Washington University

When Cooper Kupp arrived on campus, no one really knew who he was. Eastern Washington Head Coach Beau Baldwin had already determined that Kupp was going to redshirt for his freshman season, meaning he would practice with the team during the week but not play on Saturdays.

Kupp decided that he was going to major in Behavioral Economics while at EWU. He took his ideas from the classroom onto the football field. He started to look for every advantage that he could find while playing.

He started by studying three NFL receivers: Larry Fitzgerald, AJ Green, and Antonio Brown. Each receiver did something well and different. All three had different approaches to the same position.

After studying and learning from other receivers, he started to dive even deeper into every aspect of the game. He took up residence in EWU Defensive Coordinator Jeff Schmedding's office and started asking questions. He wanted to be able to see the entire game. He wanted to learn the approach a defensive coordinator would take to stop someone like him so he could be prepared to adjust.

He sat down and ate breakfast every morning with his quarterbacks, again asking questions. He wanted to know what they were looking for when they had to scramble or make a read on a defense. It was a tradition that he continued into the NFL.

His future quarterback with the Rams, Jared Goff, said of Kupp, "He has a savant-type ability to understand defenses that's greater than anyone else in the league."[xix] That ability started when he was a freshman at Eastern Washington.

Eventually, Kupp would combine his interest in behavior with his frustration over the recruiting process to create his own model for evaluating prospects. He has not shared the model with anyone yet, but his father has said that it works well.

Being undersized and a bit slow, Kupp had to find those advantages wherever he could. He started making friends with custodians at Eastern, and they allowed him into the weight room early and kept it open late for him. He started carrying around a tennis ball to help improve his catching and hand/eye coordination.

Despite not stepping on the field during his freshman season, Kupp still made an impression with the Eagles. He was named the team's Scout Team Player of the Year.

During the summer, Kupp received an honor that normally was reserved for big-time college receivers. He received an invitation to attend the prestigious Manning Quarterback Camp. The invitation was mostly a favor from Archie Manning to Kupp's grandfather, who had blocked for him with the Saints.

The family connection got Kupp in the door, but it was his talent that got him invited back year after year. He soon became a favorite target of both Manning brothers, themselves both Super Bowl MVPs.

One summer while at the camp, Peyton Manning insisted that Kupp run routes for him so that he could get ready for the season. His younger brother Eli wanted Peyton to use another receiver. The two would get into a brotherly squabble with Peyton ultimately winning. Kupp ended up running routes for Peyton Manning all afternoon long.

That argument would not have been important if it weren't for the person who overheard it. Rams General Manager Les Snead happened to be at the Manning Camp that day and overheard the argument between the brothers. He wrote a single sentence in his notepad: "Who the heck is Cooper Kupp?" He would soon find out.[xx]

The first game that Kupp played at Eastern Washington would be on the road against the 25th-ranked FBS school, Oregon State. FBS schools routinely scheduled smaller FCS schools to fill out games and to try to guarantee a win. It fills the stadium, and fans usually get to see a blowout win.

But on this day, it was not to be. Kupp caught 5 passes for 119 yards and 2 touchdowns in his college debut. The Eagles upset the heavily favored Beavers, 49-46. The Eagles followed then that up with a win over Western Oregon but lost their next two to Toledo and Sam Houston State.

What came next for the Eagles and Kupp was a thing of beauty. The team won their next eight regular season games, with Kupp dominating the competition. Kupp caught 11 passes for 205 yards against Idaho State, the team that he nearly signed with. He would catch 11 passes twice that season. He led the team in receiving yards 6 times in 12 games.

Eastern Washington finished the regular season at 10-2, good enough for the third seed in the 2013 FCS Tournament. After a first-round bye, the Eagles knocked off South Dakota State, 41-17. In the game, Kupp caught two more touchdowns, breaking the FCS record previously set by Randy Moss. It would be his 20th touchdown catch of the season, but he was not done yet.

In the quarterfinals against Jacksonville State, Eagles' quarterback Vernon Adams hit Kupp for a first-quarter touchdown pass, his 21st of the season. The Gamecocks kept the game close in the second half but the Eagles wore them down in the second half, taking the game 35-24.

"When you're facing one of the best eight teams in the country, games are going to have that choppy feel and they're not always going to be perfect," said Eastern Washington coach Beau Baldwin. "You just have to find ways to win, and our guys have been great at that."[xxi]

The semifinals saw the Eagles take on Towson University. The Tigers were the seventh seed and had just upset the second-seeded Eastern Illinois in Jimmy Garoppolo's final game with the Panthers.

Eastern Washington took a four-point lead with 1:35 left on the clock. Towson was playing with their backup quarterback after their starter had been knocked out of the game. It seemed that the Eagles were on their way to the FCS Championship game.

But in just over a minute, Towson went 71 yards to score the game-winning touchdown. EWU got the ball back with less than 30 seconds, but Adams' first pass was intercepted and the Tigers won the game, 35-31.

It was a bitter end to Kupp's redshirt freshman season. But nevertheless, it had been a successful one for him. In his first season playing college football, Kupp set six FCS records. He broke the record for receptions with 93, the record for yards with 1,691, and the record for touchdowns with 21. He won the Jerry Rice Award, an honor presented to the best FCS freshman wide receiver. He was also named first team All-American.[xxii]

Kupp had one of the best seasons in the history of college football at any level, but the question was, what would he do for his second act? The kid who could not get a college scholarship was now one of the best receivers in the country, but he always felt he needed to keep proving himself.

Unfortunately, Kupp was injured in a Week 1 win over Sam Houston State and was forced to miss the following week against Montana-Western. He returned just in time for a game at Washington, his grandfather's alma mater.

Bear in mind that Washington did not offer Kupp a scholarship when it had the chance, despite a plea from Kupp's grandfather. With that fact undoubtedly being a motivating factor, Kupp did not disappoint. He caught eight passes for 145 yards and 3 touchdowns in a 59-52 loss. The Eagles were driving for the game-tying score but a fumble ended their hopes of winning. Adams set a school record with seven touchdown passes, the most ever allowed by UW.[xxiii]

After losing to the only FBS school on their schedule, Eastern Washington got on a roll. They would win eight of their next nine games, with the only loss coming to Northern Arizona by a point. Kupp would lead the team in receiving yards in eight of those nine games.

The Eagles once again were headed back to the FCS Playoffs, this time as the fourth seed. They would host Montana, whom they had already beaten 36-26 two weeks earlier. The two schools were bitter rivals, but since he had arrived on campus, Kupp had not lost to the Grizzlies.

This time would be no exception. The Eagles rolled by Adams and Kupp's 12 receptions. After taking a 13-3 halftime lead, Eastern Washington put up 24 points in the second half for a 37-20 victory. They would then host the fifth-seed Illinois State in the quarterfinals.

The Redbirds then rolled over the Eagles on Eastern Washington's signature red turf. Eastern Illinois' offense was just too much for the Eagles' defense. The Redbirds rushed for nearly 400 yards on that day. In the fourth quarter, the Eagles were down 52-27 when Kupp and the offense tried for a valiant comeback. Kupp caught two touchdowns in the fourth quarter, but it was not enough, as Eastern Illinois went on to win the game 59-46. Kupp ended with 10 receptions for 185 yards.

His redshirt sophomore season was, in some ways, even better than his first season. For the second straight year, he was named first team All-American. He set a school record with 104 receptions, which was also the 11th-most all-time in FCS history. He had 1,431 yards and 16 touchdowns in only 12.5 games.[xxiv]

Kupp spent most of the season on the watch list for the Walter Payton Award, which is essentially the Heisman Trophy of the FCS. Past winners include Tony Romo, Steve McNair, Jimmy Garoppolo, and Trey Lance. Kupp would finish 18th in the voting for the award that year, but his time would soon come.

Having just completed two of the best seasons in NCAA history for a wide receiver, Kupp was technically eligible for the draft. In two seasons, he caught 197 passes for 3,122 yards and 37 touchdowns. Surely an NFL team would take a shot on the kid from Eastern Washington.

But changes in his life off the field would not allow Kupp to leave school just yet. Anna Croskrey and Kupp continued to date throughout their first two years in college, but the distance between them was too much for either of them to bare. She chose to leave Arkansas and enroll at EWU to be closer to Kupp.

Before she transferred, though, Kupp had already asked her to marry him. In June of 2015, just after the spring football season and semester ended, they were married in Yakima. As was the case with all Kupp family events, football was there too. Kupp would take photos at the wedding in his Eastern Washington football helmet and tuxedo.

With a new wife now on campus, Kupp stayed in college for his redshirt junior season. Anna lost some of her credits by transferring to EWU and was now starting her junior year as well. To help support the new family, Anna went to work while Kupp focused on his football career.

"A lot of people ask, 'Why did you guys get married so young? Didn't you feel you were missing out?' " Anna said. "And you're telling them, 'No, we actually think the opposite. We feel so lucky to have found someone that we love and cherish so much so early.'"[xxv]

The new season would bring more change to Kupp's life. The team's starting quarterback, Vernon Adams, transferred for his final year of eligibility to Oregon. Kupp would be working with Jordan West for the first time. The Eagles' opening game would be on the road at No. 7 Oregon, and against their former quarterback.

The Eagles ultimately lost the game but Kupp's performance will live on forever. He set the record for most receptions and receiving yards in the history of Oregon's Autzen Stadium. He caught 15 passes for 246 yards and 3 touchdowns. So, the record holder is not one of the Ducks' former receivers, but instead Eastern Washington's Cooper Kupp.

After a Week 2 loss to Northern Iowa, the Eagles rattled off six straight wins to improve to 6-2. Kupp led the team in receiving yards six times in the first eight games. But the Eagles would lose their final three games, including a blowout loss to their rival, Montana. It was the first time that Kupp had ever lost to the Grizzlies in four games. It was also the first time that Kupp and the Eagles did not qualify for the FCS Playoffs.

The season was not a total waste for Kupp, though. He set another school and FCS record with 114 catches for 1,642 yards and 19 touchdowns. He led FCS in receptions, receptions per game, yards, yards per game, and touchdowns. For the third straight season, he was a first team All-American.[xxvi]

For his efforts during the 2015 season, Cooper Kupp was also named the Walter Payton FCS College Player of the Year. He was only the second receiver to ever win the award.

Before he won the Walter Payton Award, Kupp had already announced that he would be returning to Eastern Washington for his senior season.

"I believe that God has a plan for me and a great plan for Eastern Washington. I want to be a part of that and I'm really looking forward to the offseason and getting

Eastern Washington back to a national championship,"
said Kupp.[xxvii]

Chapter 3: Senior Year & NFL Draft

Coming off a 6-5 season, Eastern Washington had a lot to prove. The team had made the FCS playoffs in Kupp's first two years but failed to do so in his redshirt junior season. Despite winning the Walter Payton Award, Kupp and his teammates had something to prove.

"I think what defines success going into his senior year is why he came back: how can he truly develop as a leader of men as a senior? How can he lead as a senior, make a difference with these guys and bring other guys the way an incredible point guard can bring everyone around them and make their team better?" Eastern Washington head coach Beau Baldwin said. "That's one of the reasons he wants to come back. He gets one shot in his life to lead as a senior in college and he's going to do it."xxviii

The Eagles opened the season on the road against Pac-12's Washington State. In his first three seasons at Eastern Washington, Kupp was 1-2 against Pac-12 teams, including an upset win over Oregon State. This would be his final chance to prove to an FBS school that he belonged at their level.

Kupp did a little bit of everything in the game. He caught 12 passes for 206 yards and 3 touchdowns, including 2 touchdowns in the third quarter when the Eagles started the quarter down by 4. He also completed a pass for 22 yards and ran the ball twice for 29 yards.

It was a tough offensive battle but in the end, the Eagles narrowly upset the heavily favored Cougars, 45-42.

"Make no mistake—it's like I said earlier in the week, Eastern Washington's first-level guys are as good as our first-level guys are," WSU coach Mike Leach said. "They proved it today and I thought they executed more discipline than we did. I think that they've done this to a lot of people, and they did it to us. Today, Cooper Kupp was the best player on the field."[xxix]

Kupp had played four games in his career against Pac-12 teams, all of whom passed on him coming out of high school. He finished his career 2-2 in those four games with 40 receptions for 716 yards and 11 touchdowns. He proved that he belonged at an elite level.

In Week 2, the Eagles traveled to take on defending FCS Champion North Dakota State. In the first half of the game, Kupp caught two touchdown passes, giving him 61 for his career. He now had the most touchdown receptions in the history of both FCS and FBS.

Unfortunately, he hurt his shoulder and was forced to miss the entire second half of the game.

The Eagles would end up losing the game in overtime, 50-44. It would be the team's last loss of the regular season. Eastern Washington cruised through the remainder of their schedule, finishing the season at 10-1. They would be the second overall seed in the FCS playoffs, behind North Dakota State.

Eastern Washington cruised to easy victories over Central Arkansas and Richmond, sending them to the semifinals against Youngstown State. Kupp did everything he could to help secure the win with 10 receptions for 180 yards and 2 touchdowns.

But he could only watch the game's final play. Eastern Washington was up by four with one second remaining on the clock. Youngstown had the ball on the Eagles' five-yard line. Penguins quarterback Hunter Wells threw a pass to junior tight end Kevin Rader in the back of the end zone.

The Eagles' defender had his back to the ball and Rader was able to pin the ball to the defender's back and, as he fell to the ground, pulled in the game-winning catch as time expired. In a strange twist of fate, Kupp's college career came to an end on a reception that wasn't his.[xxx]

"One play doesn't define the year," Baldwin said. "It was a battle to the very end. I feel so good about what this group of seniors has done."[xxxi]

Kupp finished his senior season with 117 catches for 1,700 yards and 17 touchdowns. He was once again named a first team All-American. He was the only player in the history of FCS football to be a four-time All-American. He finished second for the Walter Payton Award.

For his college career, he had an astounding 428 catches for 6,464 yards and 73 touchdowns. He set 15 FCS records, 11 Big Sky Conference records, and 26 EWU records. He was easily the most decorated receiver in the history of FCS, if not the history of college football, but now he had to prove himself all over again for the NFL scouts.[xxxii]

Kupp received an invitation to the Senior Bowl in Mobile, Alabama. This would give him the opportunity to show that he could play against some of the best players in the nation, and he did not disappoint.

Scouts were blown away by his ability to get open, break press coverage, and catch jump balls. He became one of the breakout stars of the week leading up to the game.

"He's had a fantastic week," Pro Football Focus analyst Gordon McGuinness said. "Everything he's been asked to do this week, he's done incredibly well. He's been 1-on-1 with Michigan's Jourdan Lewis—who is an incredibly good corner—a lot of times this week, and he's gotten the better of him. On slant routes, he's been utterly dominant. I think the defensive backs are going to be seeing him catching slant passes in their sleep in front of them. He's also sure at making the catch and he can match guys down the field with speed. He's a guy who has definitely opened some eyes. If teams weren't properly focused on him before now, they definitely will be in the future."[xxxiii]

The game itself was mostly an afterthought. What really mattered was how Kupp played in those practices leading up to the game. He proved that he belonged on that level.

"When I step on the field, I have an earnest belief that I'm the best who's stepped on the field," Kupp said. "I also believe there is so much more that I need to improve on, that I am not good enough yet. ... I'm never going to be stagnant or OK with any part of my game."[xxxiv]

At the NFL Draft Combine, Kupp ran a slower-than-expected 4.62 in the 40-yard dash. But they were quickly impressed with him when they sat down to interview him. Los Angeles Rams General Manager Les Snead remembered the note that he wrote one summer at the Manning Passing Camp, and the Rams spent a good amount of time with Kupp.

New head coach Sean McVay was especially impressed with him.

"You felt like you were almost talking to a receiver coach," McVay said. "You watch him play, you see he's got those pre-snap plans that, a lot of times, you don't see. He is one of the more polished college receivers that I've evaluated coming out in a while."xxxv

When Kupp left the room, McVay actually thought about hiring him as one of his assistant coaches. He turned to his new receivers coach, Eric Yarber, and told him, "You're lucky we just hired you."

Kupp also had his former coach in his corner, Beau Baldwin. Baldwin would tell anyone who would listen that Kupp was the best receiver in all of college football.

"I don't have a single doubt in my mind that he will have an amazing impact in an NFL offense," Baldwin said. "I've never seen him get defended by anyone. I've never seen him struggle. I mean, it's been consistent, no matter who we played, no matter who it's against. And he's got a drive and a mindset that he's not going to allow himself to not have success."[xxxvi]

Despite all the hype, scouts were still cautiously projecting that Kupp would go somewhere in the second or third round of the draft. But regardless, Kupp knew that he was going to be great once he got to the NFL.

"What I'm excited about is getting to a team, knowing where I'm gonna be at, knowing the players and coaches I'm gonna be around, and being able to go out and be the best player I can be and produce for a city and for a team," Kupp said before his draft night. "I believe, regardless, I can be a Hall of Fame player, and that's what I'm excited to be. That's not gonna change just because I played at a small school."[xxxvii]

In the first round of the 2017 NFL Draft, three receivers were selected in the top 10 picks. None of them would have the career that Cooper Kupp would have. Then, in the second round, the Rams held the 44th pick. They selected tight end Gerald Everett out of South Alabama.

Finally, with the fifth pick in the third round, the Los Angeles Rams selected Cooper Kupp out of Eastern Washington University.

"I've played against some very good football players," Kupp said after being drafted, "and I have played against some very good teams, as well, and I've been able to produce in both situations. I believe I prepared to be the best when I step on the field and that's not going to change moving up to the NFL. I pride myself on that preparation and what it takes to be great. If people want to question that, that's fine. I'm just going to go and do what I do and I believe that that opinion will change soon."[xxxviii]

With Cooper getting drafted, the Kupp family became just the fifth in NFL history to have three generations of players in the NFL.

"We are just so thrilled," Cooper's father, Craig, said. "He's just worked so hard for this since he was a freshman in high school. And it's so great that he'll be able to stay on the West Coast."[xxxix]

Chapter 4: Professional Career

Rookie Season

The Rams were a team in transition when Cooper Kupp arrived for training camp in 2017. A year earlier, the team played its first season in Los Angeles after moving from Saint Louis. The Rams had also traded up to the number one overall pick in the 2016 NFL Draft to select quarterback Jared Goff out of Cal.

Toward the end of the 2016 season, the Rams fired head coach Jeff Fisher. After the season ended, LA hired Sean McVay, who, at the time, was the youngest coach in NFL history.

Heading into 2017, the Rams had not had a winning season since 2003 with the "Greatest Show on Turf."

But Kupp still felt like he had to prove that he belonged on that level. Despite being the all-time leading receiver in FCS history and a third-round draft pick, Kupp still felt like the kid who did not get any FBS scholarship offers.

In his first game, he started to show what he was capable of. The Rams hosted the Indianapolis Colts to start the season. The Rams were up 10-3 in the second quarter, but their offense started to stagnate. Just when it looked like the Colts were going to start a comeback, Kupp made a spectacular juggling catch for 24 yards. LA would score four plays later to go up by two scores.

On the next drive, Kupp caught an 18-yard touchdown pass, the first of his NFL career, to put the game away early for the Rams. LA would go on to defeat the Colts, 46-9. In his pro debut, Kupp had four catches for 76 yards and a touchdown.

"I keep saying the same thing," Goff said. "Cooper did a good job and executed everything he needed to do. He's just consistent. Every day, you know what you're going to get from him."[xl]

While his numbers weren't what he had done in college, it was still a solid debut for a rookie. Kupp showed no nerves on the big stage.

"I always have nerves," Kupp said. "It doesn't matter. I've had nerves since I was 9 years old, my first time on the football field. It's always the same. It's kind of special when you have that. I don't think a lot of people get to feel that, so I embrace it."[xli]

As the weeks progressed, Kupp started building a relationship with Goff. The two continued the tradition the Kupp had started in college. Every morning, they would have breakfast together to discuss football. The problem that Kupp kept running into was that there just were not enough passes to go around.

The Rams already had established receivers in Sammy Watkins and Robert Woods. With three quality receivers on the roster as well as fellow rookie tight end Gerald Everett, Kupp just was not getting the number of targets that he was used to in college.

After starting the year 3-2, the Rams won six of seven games to take control of the NFC West. Against New Orleans in Week 12, Kupp set his then-career high with 8 catches for 116 yards. Two weeks later, he set a new career high in yards with 118 against the Eagles.

By the final week of the season, the Rams were 11-4 and had already clinched the NFC West and the third seed in the NFC. Kupp and most of the starters sat out the team's final game against the San Francisco 49ers.

Kupp ended his first full season in the league with 62 catches for a team-leading 869 yards and 5 touchdowns.[xlii]

The Rams hosted the Atlanta Falcons in the opening round of the playoffs. It was the first time in more than 14 years that the Rams hosted a playoff game.

Matt Ryan and the Falcons owned the first quarter but Aaron Donald and the Rams' defense held Atlanta to only two field goals. Finally, at the start of the second quarter, Atlanta scored the game's first touchdown to go up 13-0.

With the Falcons about to take control of the game, Kupp caught his first career touchdown pass, cutting the lead to 13-7. But that would be the first and only time the Rams would see the end zone that day.

Atlanta scored a late touchdown to put the game away, upsetting the Rams 26-13 on the road. Kupp scored the team's only touchdown and caught 8 passes for 69 yards.

It was a bitter end to his rookie season, but he proved that he belonged and had a solid start to his NFL career.

The Rise to Stardom

Los Angeles looked poised to make another run into the playoffs in 2018. The team lost wide receiver Sammy Watkins in free agency but traded for Brandin

Cooks from the New England Patriots. The team was ready to defend its NFC West title and possibly more.

The Rams started the 2018 season 3-0. Kupp would have a career game in Week 4 against the Vikings. He caught nine passes for a career-high 162 yards and his first career two-touchdown game.

In Week 5 against Seattle, Kupp was on his way to another career-record day but a concussion cut his game short. He caught 6 passes for 90 yards and a touchdown but was forced to leave the game.

The following week, Kupp only played 28 plays, and for the first time in his career, he did not catch a single pass. He suffered an MCL sprain and was forced to miss two weeks.

When Kupp returned in Week 9, the Rams were already 8-0 and on the road against the Saints. New Orleans put up 35 points in the first half on their way to a 45-35 win. Kupp was impressive in his return, catching five balls for 89 yards and a touchdown. But for the Rams, it was their first loss of the season.

"We're good. We love it. You find out about yourself when you have a little bit of adversity," Sean McVay said after the game. "I know that everybody in that locker room is going to respond the right way. Sometimes setbacks can be setups for comebacks—and that's the way we look at it."[xliii]

The Rams hosted the Seahawks the next week. In the second quarter, Kupp was taken down with a horse collar tackle, and his knee bent awkwardly. He headed to the locker room but returned to the game in the third quarter.

Late in the fourth quarter, Kupp was running a route. He brushed up against a defender, went to cut, but fell to the ground. He was helped off the field, and this time he didn't return.

The next day, Kupp had an MRI on his knee, and it revealed that he had torn his ACL. He was placed on injured reserve and missed the remainder of the season.

"It's a huge loss for our football team, he's such an important part of what we do and a great football player, a great person, and it's tough, but fortunately we've got guys that are ready to step up," McVay said.[xliv]

For Kupp, it was a devasting injury, especially given that he was just coming off another injury and was just starting to get back into shape.

"ACL is just a term in sports that—everyone knows about it—they know the implications of it," Kupp said. "(Shaquille) Griffin was on the outside, so I kind of tried to burst him vertical because he was kind of sitting on the route, burst him vertical and get him going, and as soon as I put my foot in the ground, he was able to kind of collision me a little bit and—leg hit the ground and it obviously didn't feel good. Something was wrong."[xlv]

Thus, the 2018 season would essentially be a lost season for Kupp. Over the course of his entire playing career, going all the way to high school, he was rarely injured. He missed a handful of games during his college career with a sprained shoulder but he never had any major injuries. But this season, it had been one thing after another, finally culminating in the ACL injury.

The rest of the season was a rollercoaster ride for the Rams. LA finished the regular season at 13-3 and won the NFC West for the second straight year. In the playoffs, the Rams knocked off the Cowboys and beat the Saints in the NFC Championship game on a controversial no-call pass interference play. The Rams were headed to Super Bowl LIII where they would take on the formidable New England Patriots.

The game was the lowest scoring in Super Bowl history, with the Patriots ultimately knocking off the Rams 13-3. While both teams' defenses showed why they deserved to be there, the offenses struggled. Even the legendary Patriots quarterback Tom Brady did not have his usual GOAT-like numbers, but Jared Goff had one of the worst games by a quarterback in Super Bowl history. He was 19-38 for 229 yards and an interception. He was missing wide-open receivers all game long.

It is hard *not* to wonder what would have happened if Kupp had played in the game. By this point, Kupp and Goff had developed a close relationship, and with Kupp running open, perhaps Goff would have completed more passes. But we will never know, as Kupp was watching the entire game with his knee injury.

Even before he could walk, Kupp was already back in the weight room getting ready for the 2019 season. He had Rams' rehabilitation/athletic training assistant Byron Cunningham create an upper-body workout for him so that he would not lose strength while injured.

"This injury has taught me patience. This isn't an injury where you get hurt on Sunday and you go through treatment and you are back on the field on Sunday again, as much as you want to," Kupp said. "Thinking forward to that point, it's tough with this injury. Like I've said, I always want to be looking forward, but once you get too far ahead it's tough. I'm never going to live in a state of doubt—that I don't belong here, that I'm not supposed to be here," Kupp said. "Like I said, [it's] the realization that the injury did happen and that I am where I'm supposed to be."xlvi

After four months in the weight room, Kupp was finally cleared to run and cut. Cunningham began putting him through a rigorous workout to get him back into game shape.

"I wouldn't necessarily say he is on time or on pace. Kupp is right where he needs to be," Cunningham said. "He's doing a phenomenal job with his rehab. He's a great listener, pays attention to detail and he's a hard worker and that makes my job so much easier."[xlvii]

Once again, Kupp had to prove himself to the world. Working alone on a back field, he kept pushing himself harder and harder to ensure that he would be ready for the start of the season. There was always that doubt that crept into the back of his head, but Kupp knew that he was going to come back stronger than ever.

"I feel good. I don't think we like to talk about being on pace or off pace, ahead or behind or anything like that, but I think I'm where I'm supposed to be," Kupp said. "Now, to get back on the field and put cleats on for the first time since the injury, it feels like it really just kind of refreshes things and gives me some new motivation to be able to go attack this thing."[xlviii]

In his first game back since the injury, Kupp caught 7 passes, but for only 46 yards, in a win over the Carolina Panthers. The following week, he caught 5 passes for 120 yards and a touchdown, his first since coming back.

In Week 3, the 2-0 Rams traveled to Cleveland to take on the Browns. Kupp would have his best game since his return. He caught a career-high 11 passes for 101 yards, including 2 touchdowns, the only 2 the Rams scored all game. His final touchdown came in the fourth quarter, giving the Rams a lead they would not relinquish. But in typical Kupp fashion, he passes the praise on to his quarterback.

"It mostly was Jared being able to stay alive in the pocket and making some great throws in tight windows," Kupp said. "He has a lot of trust in me, being in the right place at the right time."[xlix]

After starting the season 3-0, the Rams dropped their next three games against NFC powerhouses Seattle, Tampa Bay, and San Francisco. Despite the losses, Kupp kept putting up big numbers. In those losses, he caught 18 passes for 255 yards and 2 touchdowns.

In Week 8, Kupp set a career high with 220 yards against the Bengals. The Rams won the game in London to improve to 5-3 on the season. But after only eight games back from injury, Kupp had already set new career highs in receptions and yards and tied his career high with two touchdowns in a game.

The Rams finished the last eight games going 4-4 to finish the year at 9-7. A late-season loss to their rivals, San Francisco, ended their playoff hopes. Kupp finished this third season in the league with career highs in all categories, with 94 receptions, 1,161 yards, and 10 touchdowns.[1]

The 2020 off-season saw a bit of a transition for the Rams. The team traded its first-round pick in exchange for defensive back Jalen Ramsey and traded a later-round pick for linebacker Dante Fowler. The team also cut running back Todd Gurley. Before getting hurt, Gurley was one of the best running backs in the NFL but was slowed by injuries.

The team also traded away wide receiver Brandin Cooks. The move showed just how much faith the team had in Kupp. He was now wide receiver number one for the Rams. To show just how much faith the team had in Kupp, they reached a contract extension with him. He signed a three-year, $48-million deal to stay in Los Angeles.

"I'm obviously incredibly grateful to be here, to be able to play for a great organization," Kupp said after signing his new deal. "I love it here. I don't want to go anywhere."[li]

Now, Kupp had the pressure that comes with being the top wide receiver and with the big contract. And in the first few games of the 2020 season, it appeared that pressure was getting to him. Through the first seven games of the season, the Rams were 5-2, but Kupp only had 37 catches and two touchdowns.

In Week 8, he exploded for 11 catches for 110 yards, but the Rams lost to the Dolphins. In two losses to the

San Francisco 49ers, Kupp had a total of five catches for 52 yards. After dropping both games to the 49ers in 2020, the Rams had lost four straight to their division rival.

Despite Kupp's low touchdown numbers, the Rams kept winning. They ended the season at 10-6, good enough for the second Wild Card spot. Kupp was forced to miss the final game of the season with COVID. In 15 games, he only caught three touchdown passes, the lowest of his career, including the season he missed eight games with injuries.

In the opening round of the playoffs, the Rams traveled to Seattle to take on the NFC West champions, the Seattle Seahawks. Two weeks earlier, the Seahawks celebrated winning the division title on LA's home field. The Rams did not forget what that felt like.

From the start of the game, the Rams dominated Seattle. They won the game 30-20, but it was only a late Seattle touchdown that made the game close.

"We come up here, and all week we were told how good they are and how we snuck into the playoffs," Goff said. "Two weeks ago, you saw them smoking cigars and getting all excited about beating us, and winning the division, and we were able to come up here and beat them."[lii]

The real story of the game was Kupp limping off the field late in the game. With a little over two minutes remaining, Kupp made his way to the LA bench and did not return. At first, his injury was just called a bruised knee, but as the following week went on, the knee was not getting any better.

The injury was then said to be bursitis, which is a swelling of the fluid sack in the knee, but in the end, the injury was much more serious than even that.

"Bursitis is something I dealt with during the course of the year. At the end of the day, it really wasn't what kept me out of that last game," Kupp said. "I had something else that's a French name that's basically a de-gloving of the tissue beneath my skin. It's not a pretty thing. It was a de-gloving injury. It wasn't bursitis. I dealt with bursitis early in that year but it wasn't anything, was playing through that just fine, so I'm not too worried about that, obviously. There are some things to kind of mitigate that risk. Going into the year, have a plan to make sure we're taking care of that. This was something else that was just kind of a freaky thing that happened and it's unfortunate. It's just something that happens, can't really prevent it. Just moving forward from it."[liii]

The Rams headed to Green Bay to take on the top-seeded Packers. Two days before the game, Kupp was ruled out with a knee injury. For the second time in three seasons, Kupp was unable to play in the playoffs for the Rams.

LA would end up losing to Green Bay 32-18 without Kupp. It would be another disappointing offseason for Kupp as he rehabbed yet another knee injury.

A Super Season

With another offseason to rehab, Kupp decided to make a move. He moved his family to a suburb of Portland, Oregon. Kupp turned the tennis court in the backyard of his new house into a barn that he used to explore everything that had to do with being a wide receiver.

He had field turf put in so he could run routes, a curved treadmill for speed work, and a timing gate used to calculate his speed.

At the end of the offseason, Kupp came out of his barn fully healed and ready to smash receiving records.

"My knee is doing really well. It was such a weird injury going through the end of last year. We did everything we could coming into that last game to try to get things back on the field," he said. "I think we had 12-15 needles put into my knee that week just trying to figure out—whether it's numbing the pain or pulling fluid out—all the different things you're trying to do just to get back on the field. We honestly didn't call that until the last second in terms of I wasn't going to be able to go, which was a heartbreaker, but that thing really ended up tearing out for a good portion of the offseason, in terms of the time it took to get that thing going. It was a weekly process getting someone to come out every single day of the offseason, try to work through that so I could get back training again. But it's feeling great now, no issues with it."[liv]

Kupp was also going to have a new quarterback. In the offseason, the Rams traded Jared Goff and two first-round picks to the Detroit Lions in exchange for quarterback Matthew Stafford.

As soon as the trade took place, Kupp reached out to Stafford and the two started having breakfast together daily. Kupp had been running head coach Sean McVay's offense for five years now, and he began to teach Stafford all the ins and outs of the complicated offensive scheme.

"If you added up all the hours that those two have spent together, one-on-one in the quarterback room, in that setting outside of the scheduled meeting time, it would make up a lot of time and people probably wouldn't even believe it," said Kevin O'Connell, the Rams offensive coordinator.[lv]

After all those hours together, Stafford and Kupp developed a close relationship and an understanding of what the other was looking for on the football field.

"The more time you can spend talking about football with somebody like him that just eats it up, it's just going to be better for us," Stafford said. "I think it's been reflective in his ability to make plays for our team to help us win."[lvi]

In the first three weeks of the season, this newfound friendship paid immediate dividends for the Rams. LA started the season 3-0. Kupp caught 25 passes for 367 yards and 5 touchdowns. In three games with Stafford, he had already exceeded his touchdown total from the previous season.

After a Week 4 loss to Arizona, the Rams rattled off four straight wins to start the season 7-1. Then, after a tough loss to Tennessee, the Rams were about to face off against their rivals, San Francisco. The 49ers had beaten the Rams four-straight times at that point.

In the week between the two games, the Rams signed some receiver help for Kupp and Stafford. The team brought in Odell Beckham Jr., who had been recently cut by the Cleveland Browns. The Rams now had a legitimate deep threat to take some of the double coverages away from Kupp.

It did not help against the 49ers, though. San Fran blew out the Rams for their fifth straight win over their division rivals. After a third-straight loss to the Packers on the road, the Rams were reeling a bit. After starting the season 7-1, the team was now 7-4 and saw its lead in the division disappear.

In Week 13, the Rams traveled to Arizona to take on the division-leading Cardinals. Arizona had already beaten the Rams earlier in the season; another loss would all but eliminate LA from the division race.

Rams defensive tackle Aaron Donald dominated the game. Kupp caught a career-high 13 passes for 123 yards and a touchdown late in the third quarter that sealed the win. The Rams improved to 9-4, only one game behind the Cardinals for the division lead.

After the loss to the Rams, the Cardinals fell apart as a team. By the last week of the season, the Rams were 12-4 and had clinched the NFC West title. In the final game of the regular season, the Rams faced off against the 49ers again. San Fran needed the win to clinch a playoff berth, while the Rams were looking to spoil a division rival's season.

The Rams jumped out to an early 17-0 lead but the 49ers fought back to tie the score at 17 heading into the fourth quarter. With 2:29 left in the game, Kupp caught a go-ahead touchdown pass from Stafford. It appeared as though the Rams were about to break their losing streak against the 49ers.

But just like that, San Fran drove down the field to tie the game and send it into overtime. In overtime, Stafford threw a costly interception, and San Fran's Robbie Gould hit the game-winning field goal, sending the 49ers to the playoffs.

The Rams made the playoffs but with the loss, missed out on the second seed, which would have given them two playoff games.

"This is a tough feeling," coach Sean McVay said. "Our guys did a good job being able to navigate through the season. To be able to still win the division is a good accomplishment, but I don't know that right now is the time to celebrate that."[lvii]

The loss was the sixth in a row for the Rams against the 49ers.

For Kupp, it was the best season of his career and possibly the best season ever by a wide receiver. He became just the fourth wide receiver in NFL history to lead the league in catches, yards, and touchdowns. He ended the season with 145 catches for 1,947 yards and 16 touchdowns. It was the second-most receiving yards and receptions in a season in NFL history. For his efforts, Kupp was named the Offensive Player of the Year, first team All-Pro, and was invited to his first Pro Bowl.[lviii]

The Rams opened the playoffs with a 33-11 win over the Cardinals. Kupp caught 5 passes for 61 yards and a touchdown. In the Divisional Round, the Rams traveled to Tampa Bay to play Tom Brady and the defending Super Bowl Champions, the Buccaneers.

The Rams jumped out to a 20-3 halftime lead, and it appeared Brady would be headed home early this season. In the second quarter, Kupp managed to get behind the Bucs' defense somehow and caught a 70-yard touchdown pass from Stafford.

In the second half, Tampa Bay came storming back. After Stafford scored to bring the lead to 27-3, the Bucs scored 24 straight points to tie the game. Tampa's final score came with 42 seconds left in the game.

But just as it appeared that the game was heading to overtime, Stafford and Kupp took over. The Rams got the ball on their own 25-yard line. On the first play of the drive, Stafford was sacked for a two-yard loss, costing the Rams their final timeout.

On the very next play, Stafford connected with Kupp for a 23-yard gain to the Rams' 46-yard line. Kupp had the awareness to get out of bounds, stopping the clock. One play later, Kupp once again got behind the defense and caught a high, lofting pass down at the Tampa 12-yard line.

The Rams ran up to the ball. Stafford was able to snap the ball and spike it, stopping the clock. On the final play of the game, Matt Gay kicked a 30-yard game-winning field goal to send the Rams to the NFC Championship game.

"Man, he's the heart and soul of this offense," Stafford said of Kupp after the game. "What he's able to do down in, down out, whether it's in the pass game, run game—he's an unbelievable competitor."[lix]

Kupp finished the game with 9 receptions for 183 yards and a touchdown. On the final drive, he caught 2 passes for 63 yards to help the Rams win the game.

The Rams would get to host the NFC Championship game against their rivals, the San Francisco 49ers. By this point, the Niners had won six straight against LA and had shown no signs of weakness against the team from the City of Angels.

After a scoreless first quarter, Stafford hit Kupp for a 16-yard touchdown pass to give the Rams a 7-0 lead.

The 49ers responded with 17 straight points to take a 17-7 lead into the fourth quarter. After a fiery speech on the sideline by Rams All-Pro defensive tackle Aaron Donald, the Rams' defense did not give up another point, allowing the offense to come to life.

Early in the fourth quarter, Stafford hit Kupp again for an 11-yard touchdown pass to bring the Rams within three.

On a third and 10 with just over eight minutes remaining, Stafford hit Kupp for a 20-yard completion down to the 49ers' 25-yard line. It would set up Gay for a game-tying field goal with just over eight minutes left in the game.

With 3:26 left in the game, the Rams had a third-and-three from the 49ers' 38-yard line. Stafford connected with Kupp on a short slant and the receiver took off down the field. He was finally dragged down at the 12-yard line, setting up the game-winning field goal.

The 49ers got the ball back with 1:09 left in the game, but Donald pressured San Fran quarterback Jimmy Garoppolo into an errant throw that was intercepted by the Rams. LA was headed to the Super Bowl.

"You can't write the story any better," Stafford said. "I'm at a loss for words. I'm just having a blast playing ball with these guys and, shoot, we've got one more at the home stadium. Let's get it done."[lx]

The Rams were now headed to Super Bowl LVI, but they would not have to travel that far. LA would be just the second team in Super Bowl history to play the game in their home stadium. After 54 years without the home team ever making it to the Super Bowl, the Tampa Bay Buccaneers played in Super Bowl LV in their home stadium. Now, the Rams would get to play their Super Bowl in SoFi Stadium.

The Rams would be taking on Joe Burrow and the surprising Cincinnati Bengals. Cincinnati got to the Super Bowl by upsetting the Kansas City Chiefs and Patrick Mahomes. The Bengals had never won a Super Bowl heading into this game.

LA quickly opened up a 7-0 lead as Stafford hit Odell Beckham Jr. on a 17-yard touchdown pass. Beckham would tear his ACL just before halftime and miss most of the game. Once Beckham went down, the Bengals were able to double-team Kupp and shut him down for part of the game.

But first, Kupp would catch an 11-yard touchdown pass early in the second quarter. The Rams went for two but it failed, giving them a 13-3 lead. With five minutes remaining in the half, the Bengals scored their first touchdown to cut the Rams' lead to 13-10 going into halftime.

The third quarter belonged to the Bengals. Cincinnati was able to put up 10 points, and the Rams managed only a field goal. Heading into the fourth quarter, Cincinnati had a 20-16 lead.

The two teams couldn't manage much offense early in the fourth quarter. LA got the ball back at its own 21-yard line with just over six minutes remaining. In the nearly two quarters since Beckham was injured, Kupp only had two catches for 22 yards. But then came the final drive.

On a fourth-and-one from their own 30, Kupp took a handoff and ran for seven yards, getting a critical first down. Kupp caught three passes on the drive for 38 yards to get the ball inside the Bengals' 10-yard line.

On second and goal from the one, Stafford hit Kupp on a back-shoulder fade for the game-winning touchdown. The Rams won Super Bowl LVI 23-20.

Cooper Kupp finished the game with eight catches for 92 yards and two touchdowns. He was named the game's Most Valuable Player.

"Whatever it is, I just want to execute my job to the best of my ability," Kupp said. "I trust that as the game goes on, I will have opportunities, as well, and I just want to stay ready for those things, stay locked in."[lxi]

After the game, Kupp told reporters that he had envisioned this moment after the Rams lost the Super Bowl to the Patriots a few years earlier.

"I don't know what it was, there was just this vision that God revealed to me that we were gonna come back, we were gonna be a part of a Super Bowl and we were gonna win it," Kupp said. "And somehow, I was going to walk off the field as the MVP of the game."[lxii]

In winning the Super Bowl MVP and catching touchdowns in every postseason game the Rams played, Kupp joined some elite company. He became the second receiver to score a touchdown in four playoff games, joining Larry Fitzgerald of the Cardinals.

He also became only the second player to win Super Bowl MVP and Offensive Player of the Year in the same season, joining Joe Montana. He set the postseason record for most receptions, most touchdowns, and most receiving yards.

"And Cooper Kupp is the man," Sean McVay said after the game.[lxiii]

A Super Hangover

After reaching such heights, there is only one way to go, and that is down. The Rams spent most of the offseason celebrating their Super Bowl victory, and no one more so than Kupp.

He agreed to a five-year, $110-million extension with the Rams in the offseason. The kid out of Washington that couldn't get an FBS scholarship was now one of the highest-paid receivers in the NFL after leading the league in all receiving categories the previous season.

The Rams also agreed to bring Stafford back on a four-year, $160-million contract extension. The band was back together for another run at a championship.

But like so many teams that had won the big game before them, the Super Bowl hangover was a very real thing, and it started almost immediately. The Buffalo Bills came into SoFi just as the Rams were raising their Super Bowl banner and getting their rings.

Down 10-0 in the second quarter, Kupp and Stafford hooked up for the team's only touchdown of the night. Despite the score being tied at the half, Buffalo dominated the second half, outscoring the Rams 21-0.

"Very humbling night, but one where you look yourself in the mirror and say you have to be better," McVay said. "We weren't ready to go. That's on me. ... There were a lot of decisions I made that didn't put us in the best position to succeed. It was a very humbling night."[lxiv]

Despite the huge loss, Kupp still had 13 catches for 128 yards and a touchdown.

The Rams followed up their opening-day loss with wins over Atlanta and Arizona but dropped another regular season game to the 49ers. In the loss, Kupp set a new career-high with 14 receptions.

But the losses kept piling up, especially as the injuries started to come to key players. Both Stafford and Donald, the main pieces of both the offense and defense, missed time with injuries. Later in the season, both would be placed on injured reserve.

By Week 9, the Rams were 3-5 as they hosted the Arizona Cardinals. In the game, Kupp jumped for a pass from backup quarterback John Wolford. He landed awkwardly on his right ankle. Kupp stayed on the ground for a few minutes and was then helped to the sideline.

At first, McVay and the Rams training staff feared the worst, but it turned out to be a high ankle sprain.

However, Kupp would need surgery to repair the issue, ending his season.

"Obviously you never ever replace a player like Cooper Kupp, but we've got to figure out the best way to accentuate the skill sets of the guys that will be playing," McVay said.[lxv]

With an eight-week recovery time, Cooper Kupp's season was now over. For the second time in his six-year career, he would miss more than eight games in a season.

The Rams finished the season with a 5-12 record, the worst ever for a defending Super Bowl Champion. The team also did not have a first-round draft pick in 2023 after trading it to the Detroit Lions for Stafford.

"It certainly has been something that I don't think anyone could have predicted," McVay said the week before the season ended. "When it rains, it pours. Once this season ends, you are really able to take a step back and use the entire inventory of information that you've gathered to absolutely apply these in a tangible way that can hopefully elicit the desired results. So that these are things that you can avoid and try to say 'I never want to go through something like this ever again.'"[lxvi]

McVay has already said that he will be returning for the 2023 season, along with Kupp, Stafford, and Donald, to take another run at a second Super Bowl title.

Chapter 5: Personal Life

"Without a doubt, there's no doubt in my mind, not only would I not be here where I am today without her or accomplishing the things that I would be doing," Cooper Kupp said. "I really believe I may not be in this—I may not be in the NFL if it wasn't for her and what she has inspired in me and pushed me to do."[lxvii]

The "her" in that sentence is Cooper's wife, Anna. The two met at a track meet during their senior year of high school. Anna went to the University of Arkansas on a track scholarship, while Cooper stayed in Washington at Eastern on a football scholarship.

After two years apart, Anna transferred to Eastern Washington, and in 2015, they were married. While they were in college, Anna worked at a local restaurant and supported the two of them financially so that Cooper could concentrate on his football career.

When they were planning their wedding, Cooper had to tape a piece of paper up in the Eastern Washington locker room because Anna did not think that college students would RVSP to their wedding. Instead, all the football players had to do was sign up to attend.

After they were married, Anna and Cooper would host movie nights for the players at their apartment. When Cooper was watching game film, Anna was right there next to him watching and learning right along with him.

"We just were so aligned in terms of what our goals were and what we wanted to do moving forward and what we wanted to be about as a couple," Cooper said. "And the belief that football was the community, was the place that I was supposed to be, that we were supposed to be, and that's where God placed us."[lxviii]

On game day, Anna would sneak into the locker room and leave cookies for all the players. But she did not exactly have to sneak. The custodian had given Cooper a key so that he could work out whenever he wanted, so Anna just borrowed the key.

"Anna is his rock," said Austin Wagner, Kupp's best friend from high school. "I don't think there's a Cooper without what Anna's done for him. She's a person that really expects a lot out of the people around her and has kind of a high threshold for excellence … Cooper works harder because of that."[lxix]

After college, the married couple made their way to Los Angeles to be with the Rams. Cooper stayed in college for his redshirt senior year to stay with Anna so they could graduate together.

In July 2018, the couple welcomed their first son, Cooper Jameson Kupp, who they call June. Then, in January 2021, they welcomed their second son, Cypress Stellar Kupp.

As Cooper started breaking records and winning the Super Bowl MVP, Anna was still just amazed by his ability to do everything.

"I was telling him the other day," Anna said, as she was overcome with emotion, "I was saying I'm proud of you in all the moments. I'm proud of you when you wake up at 2 in the morning to go rock our kid, proud of you when you wake up at 4 in the morning to go watch film, and I'm proud of you when you break NFL records."[lxx]

Being a former college athlete, Anna sometimes works out with Cooper. She also participates in a women's basketball league with Matthew Stafford's wife.

Besides his work on the field, Cooper is also very active in his community. He recently donated $21,000 to the Second Harvest Food Bank, which will provide 84,000 meals to people in need.

"There are many societal issues that need our attention," said Kupp. "There is a movement for equality and justice. A movement for the fair treatment and humanitarian rights of our brothers and sisters, and our sons and daughters. It's a battle more than worthy of fighting for. There is also a battle to care for the people whose livelihood has been taken from them and their means of providing for their families stripped from them due to circumstances outside of their control. The common ground is the compassion for people who are hurting, and my family and I believe that it will be people helping people that will raise us to a better place and pull us through this time."[lxxi]

For three straight years, Cooper served as the honorary Chairman of the Taste of the Rams event. This event brings in chefs from around Los Angeles to prepare dishes for the charity that helps to raise money for the Los Angeles Food Bank. In 2022, the event raised more than $170,000 for the food bank.

Both Cooper and Anna have also worked hard to help raise money for veteran groups around the country. During the Super Bowl, Cooper released a limited-edition t-shirt with all of the proceeds going to Team Rubicon. The goal of Team Rubicon is to put military veterans to work by responding to natural disasters throughout the country.

This past year, Cooper teamed up with the Call of Duty Endowment. He wore special cleats and sold t-shirts with all the proceeds going to the endowment. Call of Duty Endowment raises money to help veterans find careers in the private sector when their military service is complete.

Besides being great on the football field, Cooper Cupp has also shown himself to be a great man, father, and husband. And when football is over for him, he will still have all of that.

Chapter 6: Legacy

Cooper Kupp's legacy in the NCAA is secure forever. He is one of the greatest receivers ever to play college football at any level. He owns pretty much every FCS record, including most touchdowns, receptions, and receiving yards. He also holds the record for most receiving yards in any division in college football. He will surely one day be in the College Football Hall of Fame.

Kupp is one of only eight receivers in the history of the NFL to be named a Super Bowl MVP. However, only three of those receivers, Lynn Swann, Jerry Rice, and Fred Biletnikoff, are in the Pro Football Hall of Fame. His two touchdowns receiving in the Super Bowl ties him for third all-time with 16 others who also scored two touchdowns. However, his receiving yards and receptions don't rank in the top 10 all-time in Super Bowl history.

Kupp has only been in the NFL for six seasons, but because he was in college for five years, he will be 30 prior to the start of the 2023 NFL season. In his six seasons, he has missed eight or more games in a season twice. So, in his six-year career, he has only played in 80 games, starting 66 of those.

After such a short time playing, it is hard to define what his legacy will be, but thus far, he is on track for a solid career. However, because of those unfortunate injuries, his numbers at this point in his career are well below some of his peers.

He ranks 199th in NFL history in receiving yards with 6,329. He ranks 165th in receptions with 508, and 176th in touchdowns with 46. With those numbers, over the course of his career, Kupp has averaged 6 receptions for 80 yards and .5 touchdowns per game.

While those stats are solid for an NFL receiver, they are not Hall-of-Fame-level numbers—yet. But bear in mind that his career is far from over. At only 30,

Cooper Kupp can expect to play at least another five years in the NFL if not longer. There is still time for him to create a lasting legacy both on and off the field. If he can stay healthy, he may very well emerge as the superstar he has already shown us he can be. But either way, there are undoubtedly many great things to come from Cooper Kupp.

Final Word/About the Author

I was born and raised in Norwalk, Connecticut. Growing up, I could often be found spending many nights watching basketball, soccer, and football matches with my father in the family living room. I love sports and everything that sports can embody. I believe that sports are one of the most genuine forms of competition, heart, and determination. I write my works to learn more about influential athletes in the hopes that from my writing, you the reader can walk away inspired to put in an equal if not greater amount of hard work and perseverance to pursue your goals. If you enjoyed *Cooper Kupp: The Inspiring Story of One of Football's Star Wide Receivers,* please leave a review! Also, you can read more of my works on *David Ortiz, Cody Bellinger, Alex Bregman, Francisco Lindor, Shohei Ohtani, Ronald Acuna Jr., Javier Baez, Jose Altuve, Christian Yelich, Max Scherzer, Mookie Betts, Pete Alonso, Clayton Kershaw, Mike Trout, Bryce Harper, Jackie Robinson, Justin Verlander,*

Derek Jeter, Ichiro Suzuki, Ken Griffey Jr., Babe Ruth, Aaron Judge, Novak Djokovic, Roger Federer, Rafael Nadal, Serena Williams, Naomi Osaka, Coco Gauff, Baker Mayfield, George Kittle, Matt Ryan, Matthew Stafford, Eli Manning, Khalil Mack, Davante Adams, Terry Bradshaw, Jimmy Garoppolo, Philip Rivers, Von Miller, Aaron Donald, Joey Bosa, Josh Allen, Mike Evans, Joe Burrow, Carson Wentz Adam Thielen, Stefon Diggs, Lamar Jackson, Dak Prescott, Patrick Mahomes, Odell Beckham Jr., J.J. Watt, Colin Kaepernick, Aaron Rodgers, Tom Brady, Russell Wilson, Peyton Manning, Drew Brees, Calvin Johnson, Brett Favre, Rob Gronkowski, Andrew Luck, Richard Sherman, Bill Belichick, Candace Parker, Skylar Diggins-Smith, A'ja Wilson, Lisa Leslie, Sue Bird, Diana Taurasi, Julius Erving, Clyde Drexler, John Havlicek, Oscar Robertson, Ja Morant, Gary Payton, Khris Middleton, Michael Porter Jr., Julius Randle, Jrue Holiday, Domantas Sabonis, Mike Conley Jr., Jerry West, Dikembe Mutombo, Fred

VanVleet, Jamal Murray, Zion Williamson, Brandon Ingram, Jaylen Brown, Charles Barkley, Trae Young, Andre Drummond, JJ Redick, DeMarcus Cousins, Wilt Chamberlain, Bradley Beal, Rudy Gobert, Aaron Gordon, Kristaps Porzingis, Nikola Vucevic, Andre Iguodala, Devin Booker, John Stockton, Jeremy Lin, Chris Paul, Pascal Siakam, Jayson Tatum, Gordon Hayward, Nikola Jokic, Bill Russell, Victor Oladipo, Luka Doncic, Ben Simmons, Shaquille O'Neal, Joel Embiid, Donovan Mitchell, Damian Lillard, Giannis Antetokounmpo, Chris Bosh, Kemba Walker, Isaiah Thomas, DeMar DeRozan, Amar'e Stoudemire, Al Horford, Yao Ming, Marc Gasol, Draymond Green, Kawhi Leonard, Dwyane Wade, Ray Allen, Pau Gasol, Dirk Nowitzki, Jimmy Butler, Paul Pierce, Manu Ginobili, Pete Maravich, Larry Bird, Kyle Lowry, Jason Kidd, David Robinson, LaMarcus Aldridge, Derrick Rose, Paul George, Kevin Garnett, Michael Jordan, LeBron James, Kyrie Irving, Klay Thompson, Stephen Curry, Kevin Durant, Russell Westbrook,

Chris Paul, Blake Griffin, Kobe Bryant, Anthony Davis, Joakim Noah, Scottie Pippen, Carmelo Anthony, Kevin Love, Grant Hill, Tracy McGrady, Vince Carter, Patrick Ewing, Karl Malone, Tony Parker, Allen Iverson, Hakeem Olajuwon, Reggie Miller, Michael Carter-Williams, James Harden, John Wall, Tim Duncan, Steve Nash, Gregg Popovich, Pat Riley, John Wooden, Steve Kerr, Brad Stevens, Red Auerbach, Doc Rivers, Erik Spoelstra, Mike D'Antoni, and *Phil Jackson* in the Kindle Store. If you love football, check out my website at claytongeoffreys.com to join my exclusive list where I let you know about my latest books and give you lots of goodies.

Like what you read? Please leave a review!

I write because I love sharing the stories of influential athletes like Cooper Kupp with fantastic readers like you. My readers inspire me to write more so please do not hesitate to let me know what you thought by leaving a review! If you love books on life, sports, or productivity, check out my website at claytongeoffreys.com to join my exclusive list where I let you know about my latest books. Aside from being the first to hear about my latest releases, you can also download a free copy of *33 Life Lessons: Success Principles, Career Advice & Habits of Successful People*. See you there!

Clayton

References

[i] Bishop, Greg. "Cooper Kupp's Approach to Greatness." Sports Illustrated. Jan. 21, 2022.

[ii] Underwood, Roger. "Yakima Valley's First Family of Football." Yakima Herald. Oct. 22, 2016.

[iii] Underwood, Roger. "Yakima Valley's First Family of Football." Yakima Herald. Oct. 22, 2016.

[iv] Allen, Jim. "Young Cooper Kupp Didn't Take Yakima by Storm, but His Perseverance was Legendary." The Spokesman-Review. Feb. 10, 2022.

[v] McLaughlin, Brian. "Cooper Kupp Poised to Make NFL History." Hero Sports.Com. Feb. 2, 2017. Web.

[vi] McLaughlin, Brian. "Cooper Kupp Poised to Make NFL History." Hero Sports.Com. Feb. 2, 2017. Web.

[vii] McLaughlin, Brian. "Cooper Kupp Poised to Make NFL History." Hero Sports.Com. Feb. 2, 2017. Web.

[viii] Allen, Jim. "Young Cooper Kupp Didn't Take Yakima by Storm, but His Perseverance was Legendary." The Spokesman-Review. Feb. 10, 2022.

[ix] Bishop, Greg. "Cooper Kupp's Approach to Greatness." Sports Illustrated. Jan. 21, 2022.

[x] Bishop, Greg. "Cooper Kupp's Approach to Greatness." Sports Illustrated. Jan. 21, 2022.

[xi] "Cooper Kupp Player Bio." Eastern Washington University.Com. 2014. Web.

[xii] Allen, Jim. "Young Cooper Kupp Didn't Take Yakima by Storm, but His Perseverance was Legendary." The Spokesman-Review. Feb. 10, 2022.

[xiii] "Cooper Kupp Player Bio." Eastern Washington University.Com. 2014. Web.

[xiv] Allen, Jim. "Young Cooper Kupp Didn't Take Yakima by Storm, but His Perseverance was Legendary." The Spokesman-Review. Feb. 10, 2022.

[xv] Aiden Gonzalez. "How Cooper Kupp Went from No College Offers to Several College Records." ESPN.Com. July 27, 2017. Web.

[xvi] Allen, Jim. "Young Cooper Kupp Didn't Take Yakima by Storm, but His Perseverance was Legendary." The Spokesman-Review. Feb. 10, 2022.

[xvii] Aiden Gonzalez. "How Cooper Kupp Went from No College Offers to Several College Records." ESPN.Com. July 27, 2017. Web.

[xviii] Thiry, Lindsey. "The Making of Cooper Kupp." ESPN.Com. Feb. 12, 2022. Web.

[xix] Bishop, Greg. "Cooper Kupp's Approach to Greatness." Sports Illustrated. Jan. 21, 2022.

[xx] Bishop, Greg. "Cooper Kupp's Approach to Greatness." Sports Illustrated. Jan. 21, 2022.

[xxi] "Eastern Washington Pulls Away to Beat Jacksonville State." ESPN.Com. Dec. 14, 2013. Web.

[xxii] "Cooper Kupp Biography." GoEags.Com. 2017. Web.

[xxiii] "Huskies Hold Off Eagles, 59-52, in Wild Win." ESPN.Com. Sept. 6, 2014. Web.

[xxiv] "Cooper Kupp Biography." GoEags.Com. 2017. Web.

[xxv] Eidell, Lynese. "Who is Cooper Kupp's Wife?" People Magazine. Sept. 23, 2022.

[xxvi] "Cooper Kupp Biography." GoEags.Com. 2017. Web.

[xxvii] Cline, Brandon. "Cooper Kupp Returning to Eastern Washington for his Senior Season." The Easterner. Nov. 30, 2015.

[xxviii] Nuanez, Colter. "Defining His Own Legacy." Skyline Sports.Com. Feb. 13, 2022. Web.

[xxix] Thorpe, Jacob. "Eastern Washington Pulls Off Big Upset Win Over Washington State." The Spokesman Review. Sept. 3, 2016.

[xxx] "Youngstown Beat E Washington 40-38 to Advance to Title Game." ESPN.Com. Dec. 17, 2016. Web.

[xxxi] Gerania, Nicholas. "Youngstown State Football Stuns EWU in FCS Semifinals with Last-Second TD." Yakima Herald-Republic. Dec. 17, 2016.

[xxxii] "Cooper Kupp Biography." GoEags.Com. 2017. Web.

[xxxiii] Stephenson, Creg. "Meet Cooper Kupp: The Most Talked-About Player in Mobile this Week." AL.Com. Jan. 27, 2017. Web.

[xxxiv] Tanier, Mike. "Cooper Kupp Emerges as a Not-so-Deep Sleeper." Bleacher Reports. Jan. 26, 2017.

[xxxv] Gonzalez, Alden. "How Cooper Kupp Went from No College Offers to Several College Records." ESPN.Com. July 27, 2017. Web.

[xxxvi] Gonzalez, Alden. "How Cooper Kupp Went from No College Offers to Several College Records." ESPN.Com. July 27, 2017. Web.

[xxxvii] Kirshner, Alex. "Rams Pick Cooper Kupp Broke NCAA Records." SBNation.Com. April 28, 2017. Web.

[xxxviii] Wang, Jack. "Rams Trade Down, Pick Gerald Everett, Cooper Kupp." Los Angeles Daily News. April 29, 2017.

[xxxix] Trinca, Mason. "Davis Grad, EWU All-American Cooper Kupp Picked in the Third Round of the NFL Draft by the Rams." Yakima Herald-Republic. April 28, 2017.

[xl] "Rams Cooper Kupp Makes Big Impact in Debut." San Gabriel Times. Sept. 11, 2017.

[xli] "Rams Cooper Kupp Makes Big Impact in Debut." San Gabriel Times.

Sept. 11, 2017.

xlii "Cooper Kupp 2017 Game Log." Pro-Football Reference.Com. 2020. Web.

xliii "Brees, Saints Hand Rams First Loss of the Season 45-35." ESPN.Com. Web. Nov 4, 2018. Web.

xliv Thiry, Lindsey. "Rams Cooper Kupp Out for the Season with Torn ACL." ESPN.Com. Nov. 12, 2018. Web.

xlv Dennis, Clarence. "Four Months After ACL Tear, Cooper Kupp is Right Where He Needs to Be." TheRams.Com. March 20, 2019. Web.

xlvi Dennis, Clarence. "Four Months After ACL Tear, Cooper Kupp is Right Where He Needs to Be." TheRams.Com. March 20, 2019. Web.

xlvii Dennis, Clarence. "Four Months After ACL Tear, Cooper Kupp is Right Where He Needs to Be." TheRams.Com. March 20, 2019. Web.

xlviii Dennis, Clarence. "Four Months After ACL Tear, Cooper Kupp is Right Where He Needs to Be." TheRams.Com. March 20, 2019. Web.

xlix "Goff Throws 2 TD Passes, Rams Hold Off Browns 20-13." ESPN.Com. Sept. 22, 2019. Web.

l "Cooper Kupp 2019 Game Logs." Pro-Football Reference.Com. 2020. Web.

li Daniels, Tim. "Cooper Kupp, Rams Agree to Reports 3-Year, $48 Million Extension." Bleach Report. Sept. 12, 2020.

lii "Rams Get the Better of Divisional Rival, Toppling Seahawks 30-20." ESPN.Com. Jan. 9, 2021. Web.

liii DaSilva, Cameron. "Cooper Kupp Opens Up About Two Knee Injuries from 2021." USA Today. June 3, 2021.

liv DaSilva, Cameron. "Cooper Kupp Opens Up About Two Knee Injuries from 2021." USA Today. June 3, 2021.

lv Morgan, Emmanuel. "How Does Cooper Kupp Always Get the Ball?" New York Times. Feb. 11, 2022.

lvi Morgan, Emmanuel. "How Does Cooper Kupp Always Get the Ball?" New York Times. Feb. 11, 2022.

lvii "49ers Clinch Playoff Berth By Holding Off Rams 27-24 in OT." ESPN.Com. Jan. 9, 2022. Web.

lviii "Cooper Kupp 2021 Game Logs." Pro-Football Reference.Com. 2020. Web.

lix "Gay's 30-Yard Field Goal Lifts Rams Over Brady, Bucs 30-27." ESPN.Com. Jan. 23, 2022. Web.

lx "Rams Rally to Super Bowl with Stunning 20-17 Win Over 49ers." CBS Sports.Com. Jan. 31, 2022. Web.

lxi Wagoner, Nick. "Los Angeles Rams Wide Receiver Cooper Kupp Named

MVP of Super Bowl LVI After 92-Yard, 2 TD Efford Vs. Bengals."
ESPN.Com. Feb. 13, 2022. Web.

[lxii] Wagoner, Nick. "Los Angeles Rams Wide Receiver Cooper Kupp Named
MVP of Super Bowl LVI After 92-Yard, 2 TD Efford Vs. Bengals."
ESPN.Com. Feb. 13, 2022. Web.

[lxiii] Wagoner, Nick. "Los Angeles Rams Wide Receiver Cooper Kupp Named
MVP of Super Bowl LVI After 92-Yard, 2 TD Efford Vs. Bengals."
ESPN.Com. Feb. 13, 2022. Web.

[lxiv] "Buffalo Bills Blow Out Champion Rams 31-10 in Season Opener."
ESPN.Com. Sept. 9, 2022. Web.

[lxv] Barshop, Sarah. "Rams WR Cooper Kupp to Have Ankle Surgery, Will
Go on IR." ESPN.Com. Nov. 15, 2022. Web.

[lxvi] Williams, Eric. "Free Falling: Rams on Pace For Worst Super Bowl
Hangover in NFL History." Fox Sports.Com. Jan. 17, 2023. Web.

[lxvii] Thiry, Lindsey. "The Making of Cooper Kupp." ESPN.Com. Feb. 12,
2022. Web.

[lxviii] Thiry, Lindsey. "The Making of Cooper Kupp." ESPN.Com. Feb. 12,
2022. Web.

[lxix] Thiry, Lindsey. "The Making of Cooper Kupp." ESPN.Com. Feb. 12,
2022. Web.

[lxx] Thiry, Lindsey. "The Making of Cooper Kupp." ESPN.Com. Feb. 12,
2022. Web.

[lxxi] Isaacs, Chase. "Cooper Kupp Provides 84,000 Meals for Food Banks
Serving Residents in Los Angeles, Ventura County, and Hometown Region."
The Rams.Com. July 17, 2020. Web.

Made in the USA
Las Vegas, NV
16 December 2023

82944606R00066